Contents

PHILADELPHIA Cream Cheese
Tips for the Perfect Cheesecake

For best quality and results, always use PHILADELPHIA Cream Cheese.

Preheating the oven: The baking time indicated in a recipe is based on using a preheated oven. Turn the oven on when you start to mix the cheesecake ingredients. This should allow enough time for the oven to heat to the correct temperature for when you are ready to place the cheesecake in the oven to bake. Unless otherwise indicated, always bake cheesecakes in the center of the middle oven rack.

Beating the batter: While adding ingredients, do not overbeat the cheesecake batter. Too much air beaten into the batter will result in a cheesecake that sinks in the center when cooled.

Baking cheesecakes: Overbaked cheesecakes tend to crack. Remove the cheesecake from oven when center is almost set (i.e., center of cheesecake still wiggles when pan is gently shaken from side-to-side). Although the cheesecake appears underbaked, the residual heat in the cheesecake will be enough to finish baking the center. After chilling, the cheesecake will have a perfectly smooth consistency.

Cooling cheesecakes: Cool cheesecakes completely before refrigerating. Placing a warm cheesecake in the refrigerator will cause condensation to form on the cake, resulting in a soggy cheesecake.

Cutting cheesecakes: Cut cheesecakes when they are cold rather than warm. Use a sharp knife with a clean, thin blade. To make clean cuts, dip the knife in hot water after each cut and wipe the blade clean.

For all of your occasions, PHILLY MAKES A BETTER CHEESECAKE.

During tests of plain New York-style cheesecake made with
PHILADELPHIA Cream Cheese versus store-branded cream cheese,
consumers rated PHILLY cheesecake as better tasting.

Cheesecake Favorites

AN ARRAY OF TIMELESS FAMILY FAVORITES

caramel-nut cheesecake

PREP: 20 min. | TOTAL: 5 hours 25 min. (incl. refrigerating) | MAKES: 16 servings.

▸ what you need!

2 cups HONEY MAID Graham Cracker Crumbs

1 cup PLANTERS COCKTAIL Peanuts, chopped, divided

1¼ cups sugar, divided

6 Tbsp. butter or margarine, melted

4 pkg. (8 oz. each) PHILADELPHIA Cream Cheese, softened

2 tsp. vanilla

1 cup BREAKSTONE'S or KNUDSEN Sour Cream

4 eggs

¼ cup caramel ice cream topping

▸ make it!

HEAT oven to 350°F.

1. **LINE** 13×9-inch pan with foil, with ends of foil extending over sides. Mix crumbs, ½ cup nuts, ¼ cup sugar and butter; press onto bottom of pan. Bake 10 min.

2. **MEANWHILE,** beat cream cheese, remaining sugar and vanilla with mixer until well blended. Add sour cream; mix well. Add eggs, 1 at a time, beating after each just until blended. Pour over crust.

3. **BAKE** 35 min. or until center is almost set; cool completely. Refrigerate 4 hours. Top with remaining nuts and caramel topping. Use foil handles to lift cheesecake from pan before cutting to serve.

SPECIAL EXTRA:
Cut chilled cheesecake into 16 bars, then cut each diagonally in half. Stack 2 on each dessert plate to serve.

HOW TO AVOID CRACKED CHEESECAKES:
After adding the eggs, be careful not to overbeat the batter since this can cause the baked cheesecake to crack.

PHILADELPHIA
classic cheesecake

PREP: 20 min. | TOTAL: 5 hours 45 min. (incl. refrigerating) | MAKES: 16 servings.

▶ what you need!

1½ cups HONEY MAID Graham Cracker Crumbs

3 Tbsp. sugar

⅓ cup butter or margarine, melted

4 pkg. (8 oz. each) PHILADELPHIA Cream Cheese, softened

1 cup sugar

1 tsp. vanilla

4 eggs

▶ make it!

HEAT oven to 325°F.

1. **MIX** crumbs, 3 Tbsp. sugar and butter; press onto bottom of 9-inch springform pan.

2. **BEAT** cream cheese, 1 cup sugar and vanilla with mixer until well blended. Add eggs, 1 at a time, mixing on low speed after each just until blended. Pour over crust.

3. **BAKE** 55 min. or until center is almost set. Loosen cake from rim of pan; cool before removing rim. Refrigerate 4 hours.

SIZE-WISE:
Sweets can add enjoyment to a balanced diet, but remember to keep tabs on portions.

SPECIAL EXTRA:
Top with fresh fruit just before serving.

pumpkin-swirl cheesecake

PREP: 20 min. | TOTAL: 5 hours 35 min. (incl. refrigerating) | MAKES: 16 servings.

▶ what you need!

25 NABISCO Ginger Snaps, finely crushed (about 1½ cups)

½ cup finely chopped PLANTERS Pecans

¼ cup (½ stick) butter, melted

4 pkg. (8 oz. each) PHILADELPHIA Cream Cheese, softened

1 cup sugar, divided

1 tsp. vanilla

4 eggs

1 cup canned pumpkin

1 tsp. ground cinnamon

¼ tsp. ground nutmeg

　Dash ground cloves

▶ make it!

HEAT oven to 325°F.

1. **MIX** crumbs, nuts and butter; press onto bottom of 13×9-inch pan.

2. **BEAT** cream cheese, ¾ cup sugar and vanilla with mixer until blended. Add eggs, 1 at a time, beating after each just until blended. Remove 1½ cups batter. Stir remaining sugar, pumpkin and spices into remaining batter.

3. **SPOON** half the pumpkin batter into crust; top with spoonfuls of half the plain batter. Repeat layers; swirl with knife.

4. **BAKE** 45 min. or until center is almost set. Cool completely. Refrigerate 4 hours.

HOW TO BAKE CHEESECAKE IN SPRINGFORM PAN:
If using a 9-inch springform pan, prepare and bake cheesecake as directed, increasing the baking time to 1 hour or until center is almost set.

PHILADELPHIA
new york cheesecake

PREP: 15 min. | TOTAL: 5 hours 25 min. (incl. refrigerating) | MAKES: 16 servings.

▶ what you need!

20 OREO Cookies, finely crushed (about 2¼ cups)

3 Tbsp. butter or margarine, melted

5 pkg. (8 oz. each) PHILADELPHIA Cream Cheese, softened

1 cup sugar

3 Tbsp. all-purpose flour

1 Tbsp. vanilla

1 cup BREAKSTONE'S or KNUDSEN Sour Cream

4 eggs

1 can (21 oz.) cherry pie filling

▶ make it!

HEAT oven to 325°F.

1.

2.

3.

LINE 13×9-inch pan with foil, with ends of foil extending over sides. Mix crumbs and butter; press onto bottom of pan.

BEAT cream cheese, sugar, flour and vanilla with mixer until well blended. Add sour cream; mix well. Add eggs, 1 at a time, mixing on low speed after each just until blended. Pour over crust.

BAKE 40 min. or until center is almost set. Cool completely. Refrigerate 4 hours. Use foil handles to lift cheesecake from pan before cutting to serve. Top with pie filling.

PHILLY brownie cheesecake

PREP: 10 min. | TOTAL: 6 hours (incl. refrigerating) | MAKES: 16 servings.

▶ what you need!

1 pkg. (19 to 21 oz.) brownie mix (13×9-inch pan size)

4 pkg. (8 oz. each) PHILADELPHIA Cream Cheese, softened

1 cup sugar

1 tsp. vanilla

½ cup BREAKSTONE'S or KNUDSEN Sour Cream

3 eggs

2 squares BAKER'S Semi-Sweet Chocolate

▶ make it!

HEAT oven to 325°F.

1. **PREPARE** brownie batter as directed on package; pour into 13×9-inch pan sprayed with cooking spray. Bake 25 min. or until top is shiny and center is almost set.

2. **MEANWHILE,** beat cream cheese, sugar and vanilla in large bowl with mixer until well blended. Add sour cream; mix well. Add eggs, 1 at a time, mixing on low speed after each just until blended. Gently pour over brownie layer in pan. (Filling will come almost to top of pan.)

3. **BAKE** 40 min. or until center is almost set. Run knife or metal spatula around rim of pan to loosen sides; cool. Refrigerate 4 hours.

4. **MELT** chocolate squares as directed on package; drizzle over cheesecake. Refrigerate 15 min. or until chocolate is firm.

SIZE-WISE:
Balance your food choices throughout the day so you can enjoy a serving of this rich-and-indulgent cheesecake with your loved ones.

PHILADELPHIA
chocolate-vanilla swirl cheesecake

PREP: 15 min. | TOTAL: 5 hours 25 min. (incl. refrigerating) | MAKES: 16 servings.

▸ what you need!

20 OREO Cookies, crushed (about 2 cups)

3 Tbsp. butter, melted

4 pkg. (8 oz. each) PHILADELPHIA Cream Cheese, softened

1 cup sugar

1 tsp. vanilla

1 cup BREAKSTONE'S or KNUDSEN Sour Cream

4 eggs

6 squares BAKER'S Semi-Sweet Chocolate, melted, cooled

▸ make it!

HEAT oven to 325°F.

1. **MIX** crumbs and butter; press onto bottom of foil-lined 13×9-inch pan. Bake 10 min.

2. **BEAT** cream cheese, sugar and vanilla in large bowl with mixer until well blended. Add sour cream; mix well. Add eggs, 1 at a time, mixing after each just until blended.

3. **RESERVE** 1 cup batter. Stir chocolate into remaining batter; pour over crust. Top with spoonfuls of reserved plain batter.

4. **SWIRL** batters with knife. Bake 40 min. or until center is almost set. Cool. Refrigerate 4 hours.

SPECIAL EXTRA:
Garnish with chocolate curls just before serving. Use a vegetable peeler to shave the side of an additional square of BAKER'S Semi-Sweet Chocolate until desired amount of curls are obtained. Wrap remaining chocolate and store at room temperature for another use.

NOTE:
Use foil handles to remove chilled cheesecake from pan before cutting to serve.

PHILADELPHIA double-chocolate cheesecake

PREP: 20 min. | TOTAL: 5 hours 35 min. (incl. refrigerating) | MAKES: 16 servings.

▶ what you need!

24 OREO Cookies, crushed (about 2 cups)

¼ cup (½ stick) butter or margarine, melted

4 pkg. (8 oz. each) PHILADELPHIA Cream Cheese, softened

1 cup sugar

2 Tbsp. all-purpose flour

1 tsp. vanilla

1 pkg. (8 squares) BAKER'S Semi-Sweet Chocolate, melted, slightly cooled

4 eggs

▶ make it!

HEAT oven to 325°F.

1. **MIX** crumbs and butter; press onto bottom of 13×9-inch foil-lined pan. Bake 10 min.

2. **BEAT** cream cheese, sugar, flour and vanilla with mixer until well blended. Add chocolate; mix well. Add eggs, 1 at a time, mixing on low speed after each just until blended. Pour over crust.

3. **BAKE** 45 min. or until center is almost set. Cool completely. Refrigerate 4 hours. Use foil to lift cheesecake from pan.

SIZE-WISE:
Need a sweet treat to serve a crowd? Try this rich, chocolatey dessert! Since it serves 16 people, it easily fits the bill.

HOW TO PRESS CRUMB MIXTURE INTO PAN TO MAKE CRUST:
Use bottom of dry measuring cup to press crumb mixture onto bottom of pan.

SPECIAL EXTRA:
Add ¼ cup hazelnut-flavored liqueur with the melted chocolate.

SPECIAL EXTRA:
Garnish with sifted powdered sugar and mixed berries just before serving.

PHILADELPHIA white chocolate-peppermint cheesecake

PREP: 15 min. | TOTAL: 5 hours 35 min. (incl. refrigerating) | MAKES: 16 servings.

▶ what you need!

1½ cups HONEY MAID Graham Cracker Crumbs

3 Tbsp. sugar

¼ cup (½ stick) butter, melted

4 pkg. (8 oz. each) PHILADELPHIA Cream Cheese, softened

1 cup sugar

¼ tsp. peppermint extract

1 cup BREAKSTONE'S or KNUDSEN Sour Cream

4 squares BAKER'S White Chocolate, melted

4 eggs

1 cup thawed COOL WHIP Whipped Topping

16 starlight mints

▶ make it!

HEAT oven to 325°F.

1. **LINE** 13×9-inch pan with foil, with ends extending over sides of pan. Mix crumbs, 3 Tbsp. sugar and butter; press onto bottom of pan. Bake 10 min.

2. **BEAT** cream cheese, 1 cup sugar and extract in large bowl with mixer until well blended. Add sour cream and chocolate; mix well. Add eggs, 1 at a time, mixing on low speed after each just until blended. Pour over crust.

3. **BAKE** 40 min. or until center is almost set. Cool. Refrigerate 4 hours. Use foil handles to lift cheesecake from pan before cutting to serve. Top each piece with a dollop of COOL WHIP and a mint just before serving.

SERVING SUGGESTION:
This is a great dessert to share at a holiday party. At 16 servings, there's enough for a crowd.

ultimate turtle cheesecake

PREP: 30 min. | TOTAL: 6 hours 10 min. (incl. refrigerating) | MAKES: 16 servings.

▶ what you need!

2 cups OREO Chocolate Cookie Crumbs

6 Tbsp. butter or margarine, melted

1 pkg. (14 oz.) KRAFT Caramels

½ cup milk

1 cup chopped PLANTERS Pecans

3 pkg. (8 oz. each) PHILADELPHIA Cream Cheese, softened

¾ cup sugar

1 Tbsp. vanilla

3 eggs

2 squares BAKER'S Semi-Sweet Chocolate

▶ make it!

HEAT oven to 325°F.

1. **MIX** crumbs and butter; press onto bottom and 2 inches up sides of 9-inch springform pan.

2. **MICROWAVE** caramels and milk in small microwaveable bowl on HIGH 3 min. or until caramels are completely melted, stirring after each minute. Stir in nuts; pour half into crust. Refrigerate 10 min. Refrigerate remaining caramel mixture for later use.

3. **BEAT** cream cheese, sugar and vanilla with mixer until well blended. Add eggs, 1 at a time, mixing on low speed after each just until blended. Pour over caramel layer in crust.

4. **BAKE** 1 hour 5 min. to 1 hour 10 min. or until center is almost set. Run knife around rim of pan to loosen cake; cool before removing rim. Refrigerate 4 hours.

5. **MICROWAVE** reserved caramel mixture 1 min.; stir. Pour over cheesecake. Melt chocolate as directed on package; drizzle over cheesecake.

chocolate chunk cheesecake

PREP: 10 min. | TOTAL: 4 hours 45 min. (incl. refrigerating) | MAKES: 16 servings.

▶ what you need!

18 OREO Cookies, crushed (about 1½ cups)

¼ cup (½ stick) butter, melted

3 pkg. (8 oz. each) PHILADELPHIA Cream Cheese, softened

¾ cup sugar

½ cup BREAKSTONE'S or KNUDSEN Sour Cream

3 eggs

1½ pkg. (12 squares) BAKER'S Semi-Sweet Chocolate, divided

½ cup whipping cream

▶ make it!

HEAT oven to 350°F.

1. **MIX** crumbs and butter; press onto bottom of 9-inch springform pan.

2. **BEAT** cream cheese and sugar in large bowl with mixer until well blended. Add sour cream; mix well. Add eggs, 1 at a time, beating on low speed after each just until blended. Chop 8 chocolate squares; stir into batter. Pour over crust.

3. **BAKE** 45 to 50 min. or until center is almost set. Run knife around rim of pan to loosen cake. Cool completely.

4. **BRING** cream to simmer in small saucepan on low heat. Meanwhile, chop remaining chocolate squares. Remove pan from heat. Add chocolate; stir until completely melted. Cool slightly. Pour over cheesecake. Refrigerate 3 hours. Remove rim of pan before serving cheesecake.

SIZE-WISE:
Enjoy a serving of this decadent dessert on special occasions.

HOW TO SOFTEN CREAM CHEESE:
Place completely unwrapped packages of cream cheese in microwaveable bowl. Microwave on HIGH 30 sec. or until slightly softened.

scrumptious apple-pecan cheesecake

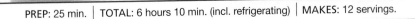

PREP: 25 min. | TOTAL: 6 hours 10 min. (incl. refrigerating) | MAKES: 12 servings.

▶ what you need!

1 cup HONEY MAID Graham Cracker Crumbs

¾ cup finely chopped PLANTERS Pecans, divided

3 Tbsp. sugar

1 tsp. ground cinnamon, divided

¼ cup (½ stick) butter or margarine, melted

2 pkg. (8 oz. each) PHILADELPHIA Cream Cheese, softened

½ cup sugar

½ tsp. vanilla

2 eggs

⅓ cup sugar

4 cups thin peeled apple slices

▶ make it!

HEAT oven to 325°F.

1. **MIX** crumbs, ½ cup nuts, 3 Tbsp. sugar, ½ tsp. cinnamon and butter; press onto bottom of 9-inch springform pan. Bake 10 min.

2. **BEAT** cream cheese, ½ cup sugar and vanilla with mixer until well blended. Add eggs, 1 at a time, beating on low speed after each just until blended. Pour over crust. Mix ⅓ cup sugar and remaining cinnamon in large bowl. Add apples; toss to coat. Spoon over cream cheese layer; sprinkle with remaining nuts.

3. **BAKE** 1 hour 10 min. to 1 hour 15 min. or until center is almost set. Run knife around rim of pan to loosen cake; cool before removing rim. Refrigerate 4 hours.

SIZE-WISE:
Enjoy a serving of this rich-and-indulgent treat on special occasions.

COOKING KNOW-HOW:
For best results, use firm apples, such as Granny Smith or McIntosh.

Cakes,
Cookies
& Pies

**CROWD-PLEASING TREATS
TO ENJOY YEAR-ROUND**

peanut butter cup pie

PREP: 15 min. | TOTAL: 4 hours 15 min. (incl. refrigerating) | MAKES: 10 servings.

▶ what you need!

1 pkg. (8 oz.) PHILADELPHIA Cream Cheese, softened

½ cup plus 1 Tbsp. creamy peanut butter, divided

1 cup cold milk

1 pkg. (3.4 oz.) JELL-O Vanilla Flavor Instant Pudding

2½ cups thawed COOL WHIP Whipped Topping, divided

1 OREO Pie Crust (6 oz.)

3 squares BAKER'S Semi-Sweet Chocolate

▶ make it!

1. **BEAT** cream cheese and ½ cup peanut butter until well blended. Add milk and dry pudding mix; beat 2 min. Whisk in 1 cup COOL WHIP; spoon into crust. Refrigerate until ready to use.

2. **MEANWHILE,** microwave remaining COOL WHIP and chocolate in microwaveable bowl on HIGH 1½ to 2 min. or until chocolate is completely melted and mixture is well blended, stirring after each minute. Cool completely.

3. **SPREAD** chocolate mixture over pudding layer in crust. Microwave remaining peanut butter in small microwaveable bowl 30 sec.; stir. Drizzle over pie. Refrigerate 4 hours or until firm.

SUBSTITUTE:
Prepare using JELL-O Chocolate Instant Pudding.

double-layer pumpkin cheesecake

PREP: 10 min. | TOTAL: 3 hours 50 min. (incl. refrigerating) | MAKES: 8 servings.

▶ what you need!

2 pkg. (8 oz. each) PHILADELPHIA Fat Free Cream Cheese, softened

½ cup sugar

½ tsp. vanilla

2 eggs

½ cup canned pumpkin

¼ tsp. ground cinnamon

Dash ground nutmeg

⅓ cup HONEY MAID Graham Cracker Crumbs

½ cup thawed COOL WHIP Sugar Free Whipped Topping

▶ make it!

HEAT oven to 325°F.

1.

BEAT cream cheese, sugar and vanilla with mixer until well blended. Beat in eggs, 1 at a time, just until blended. Remove 1 cup batter; place in medium bowl. Stir in pumpkin and spices.

2.

SPRAY 9-inch pie plate with cooking spray; sprinkle bottom with crumbs.

3.

TOP with layers of plain and pumpkin batters. Bake 40 min. or until center is almost set. Cool completely. Refrigerate 3 hours. Serve topped with COOL WHIP.

STORAGE KNOW-HOW:
Once thawed, refrigerate COOL WHIP Whipped Topping for up to 2 weeks or re-freeze.

PHILADELPHIA 3-step white chocolate raspberry swirl cheesecake

PREP: 10 min. | TOTAL: 3 hours 50 min. (incl. refrigerating) | MAKES: 8 servings.

▶ what you need!

2 pkg. (8 oz. each) PHILADELPHIA Cream Cheese, softened

½ cup sugar

½ tsp. vanilla

2 eggs

3 squares BAKER'S White Chocolate, melted

1 OREO Pie Crust (6 oz.)

3 Tbsp. raspberry preserves

▶ make it!

HEAT oven to 350°F.

1. **BEAT** cream cheese, sugar and vanilla with mixer until well blended. Add eggs; mix just until blended. Stir in chocolate. Pour into crust.

2. **MICROWAVE** preserves in small bowl on HIGH 15 sec. or until melted. Dot top of cheesecake with small spoonfuls of preserves; swirl gently with knife.

3. **BAKE** 35 to 40 min. or until center is almost set. Cool. Refrigerate 3 hours.

SIZE-WISE:
Serve this rich-and-indulgent dessert on a holiday or special occasion.

mud pie

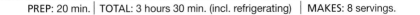

PREP: 20 min. | TOTAL: 3 hours 30 min. (incl. refrigerating) | MAKES: 8 servings.

▶ what you need!

22 NILLA Wafers, crushed (about ¾ cup)

½ cup finely chopped PLANTERS Pecans

2 Tbsp. butter, melted

1 pkg. (8 oz.) PHILADELPHIA Cream Cheese, softened

¾ cup powdered sugar

1½ cups thawed COOL WHIP Whipped Topping, divided

1 pkg. (3.9 oz.) JELL-O Chocolate Instant Pudding

1¾ cups cold milk

▶ make it!

HEAT oven to 375°F.

1. **MIX** crumbs, nuts and butter; press onto bottom and up sides of 9-inch pie plate. Bake 10 min.; cool.

2. **BEAT** cream cheese and sugar in medium bowl with mixer until well blended. Gently stir in 1 cup COOL WHIP; spread onto bottom of crust. Beat pudding mix and milk with whisk 2 min.; spoon over cream cheese layer.

3. **REFRIGERATE** several hours or until set. Top with remaining COOL WHIP just before serving.

HOW TO THAW COOL WHIP:
Place unopened tub in refrigerator. An 8-oz. tub will be completely thawed in 4 hours. Do not thaw in the microwave.

luscious four-layer
pumpkin cake

PREP: 20 min. | TOTAL: 1 hour 50 min. (incl. cooling) | MAKES: 16 servings.

▶ what you need!

1 pkg. (2-layer size) yellow cake mix

1 can (15 oz.) pumpkin, divided

½ cup milk

⅓ cup oil

4 eggs

1½ tsp. pumpkin pie spice, divided

1 pkg. (8 oz.) PHILADELPHIA Cream Cheese, softened

1 cup powdered sugar

1 tub (8 oz.) COOL WHIP Whipped Topping, thawed

¼ cup caramel ice cream topping

¼ cup PLANTERS Pecan Halves

▶ make it!

HEAT oven to 350°F.

1. **BEAT** cake mix, 1 cup pumpkin, milk, oil, eggs and 1 tsp. spice in large bowl with mixer until well blended. Pour into 2 greased and floured 9-inch round pans.

2. **BAKE** 28 to 30 min. or until toothpick inserted in centers comes out clean. Cool in pans 10 min. Remove from pans to wire racks; cool completely. Beat cream cheese in small bowl with mixer until creamy. Add sugar, remaining pumpkin and spice; mix well. Gently stir in COOL WHIP.

3. **CUT** each cake layer horizontally in half with serrated knife; stack on serving plate, spreading cream cheese filling between layers. (Do not frost top layer.) Drizzle with caramel topping just before serving; sprinkle with nuts. Refrigerate leftovers.

SIZE-WISE:
Celebrate and enjoy a serving of this indulgent cake on a special occasion.

red velvet cupcakes

PREP: 15 min. | TOTAL: 1 hour 10 min. (incl. cooling) | MAKES: 24 servings.

▶ what you need!

1 pkg. (2-layer size) red velvet cake mix

1 pkg. (3.9 oz.) JELL-O Chocolate Instant Pudding

1 pkg. (8 oz.) PHILADELPHIA Cream Cheese, softened

½ cup (1 stick) butter or margarine, softened

1 pkg. (16 oz.) powdered sugar (about 4 cups)

1 cup thawed COOL WHIP Whipped Topping

1 square BAKER'S White Chocolate, shaved into curls

▶ make it!

1.

PREPARE cake batter and bake as directed on package for 24 cupcakes, blending dry pudding mix into batter before spooning into prepared muffin cups. Cool.

2.

MEANWHILE, beat cream cheese and butter in large bowl with mixer until well blended. Gradually beat in sugar. Whisk in COOL WHIP. Spoon 1½ cups into small freezer-weight resealable plastic bag; seal bag; cut small corner off bottom of bag.

3.

INSERT tip of bag into top of each cupcake to pipe about 1 Tbsp. frosting into center of cupcake. Frost cupcakes with remaining frosting. Top with chocolate curls. Keep refrigerated.

HOW TO MAKE CHOCOLATE CURLS:
Warm a square of BAKER'S Baking Chocolate by microwaving it, unwrapped, on HIGH for a few seconds or just until you can smudge the chocolate with your thumb. Hold the square steadily and draw a peeler slowly over flat bottom of square, allowing a thin layer of chocolate to curl as it is peeled off the bottom of the square to make long, delicate curls. Use the same technique along the narrow side of the square to make short curls.

banana-sour cream cake

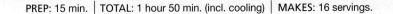

PREP: 15 min. | TOTAL: 1 hour 50 min. (incl. cooling) | MAKES: 16 servings.

▶ what you need!

1 pkg. (2-layer size) yellow cake mix

3 eggs

1 cup mashed ripe bananas (about 3)

1 cup BREAKSTONE'S or KNUDSEN Sour Cream

¼ cup oil

1 pkg. (8 oz.) PHILADELPHIA Cream Cheese, softened

½ cup (1 stick) butter, softened

1 pkg. (16 oz.) powdered sugar

1 cup finely chopped PLANTERS Walnuts

▶ make it!

HEAT oven to 350°F.

1. **BEAT** first 5 ingredients with mixer on low speed just until moistened, stopping frequently to scrape bottom and side of bowl. Beat on medium speed 2 min. Pour into greased and floured 13×9-inch pan.

2. **BAKE** 35 min. or until toothpick inserted in center comes out clean. Cool completely.

3. **BEAT** cream cheese and butter with mixer until well blended. Gradually add sugar, beating well after each addition.

4. **REMOVE** cake from pan. Carefully cut cake crosswise in half using serrated knife. Place 1 cake half, top-side down, on plate; spread with some of the cream cheese frosting. Top with remaining cake half, top-side up. Spread top and sides with remaining frosting. Press nuts into sides. Keep refrigerated.

SUBSTITUTE:
Prepare using BREAKSTONE'S Reduced Fat or KNUDSEN Light Sour Cream.

HOW TO NEATLY FROST THE CAKE:
Freeze cake layers about 20 min. before frosting. This helps to set the crumbs on the cut edges of the cake layers so they don't pull up into the frosting. And don't worry if the frosting does not look perfect on the sides of the cake—the nuts will cover any imperfections.

chocolate-raspberry thumbprints

PREP: 20 min. | TOTAL: 45 min. (incl. refrigerating) | MAKES: 4½ doz. or 27 servings, 2 cookies each.

▶ what you need!

2 cups all-purpose flour

1 tsp. baking soda

¼ tsp. salt

4 squares BAKER'S Unsweetened Chocolate

½ cup (1 stick) butter

1 pkg. (8 oz.) PHILADELPHIA Cream Cheese, softened

1¼ cups sugar, divided

1 egg

1 tsp. vanilla

⅓ cup red raspberry jam

▶ make it!

HEAT oven to 375°F.

1. **MIX** flour, baking soda and salt; set aside. Microwave chocolate and butter in large microwaveable bowl on HIGH 2 min.; stir until chocolate is completely melted. Whisk in cream cheese. Add 1 cup sugar, egg and vanilla; mix well. Stir in flour mixture. Refrigerate 15 min.

2. **ROLL** dough into 1-inch balls; coat with remaining sugar. Place, 2 inches apart, on baking sheets. Press your thumb into center of each ball; fill each indentation with about ¼ tsp. jam.

3. **BAKE** 8 to 10 min. or until lightly browned. Cool 1 min. on baking sheets; transfer to wire racks. Cool completely.

SIZE-WISE:
Dessert can be a part of a balanced diet, but remember to keep tabs on portions.

PHILADELPHIA marble
brownies

PREP: 20 min. | TOTAL: 1 hour | MAKES: 32 servings.

▶ what you need!

- 1 pkg. (19 to 21 oz.) brownie mix (13×9-inch pan size)
- 1 pkg. (8 oz.) PHILADELPHIA Cream Cheese, softened
- ⅓ cup sugar
- 1 egg
- ½ tsp. vanilla
- ½ cup BAKER'S Semi-Sweet Chocolate Chunks

▶ make it!

HEAT oven to 350°F.

1. **PREPARE** brownie batter as directed on package; spread into greased 13×9-inch pan.

2. **BEAT** cream cheese with mixer until creamy. Add sugar, egg and vanilla; mix well. Drop by tablespoonfuls over brownie batter; swirl with knife. Top with chocolate chunks.

3. **BAKE** 35 to 40 min. or until cream cheese mixture is lightly browned. Cool completely before cutting to serve. Keep refrigerated.

NOTE:
For best results, do not use brownie mix with a syrup pouch.

SUBSTITUTE:
Prepare using PHILADELPHIA Neufchâtel Cheese.

VARIATION:
Prepare as directed, omitting the chocolate chunks.

SPECIAL EXTRA:
After brownies have cooled, use a small round cookie cutter, about 1 inch in diameter, to cut small, delicate petit-four-type brownies.

sugar cookie cutouts

PREP: 20 min. | TOTAL: 1 hour 2 min. (incl. refrigerating) | MAKES: about 3½ doz. or 21 servings, 2 cookies each.

▶ what you need!

1 pkg. (8 oz.) PHILADELPHIA Cream Cheese, softened

¾ cup (1½ sticks) butter, softened

1 cup granulated sugar

2 tsp. vanilla

2¼ cups all-purpose flour

½ tsp. baking soda

¼ cup colored sugar or festive sprinkles

▶ make it!

1. **BEAT** first 4 ingredients in large bowl with mixer until well blended. Add flour and baking soda; mix well. Refrigerate 30 min.

2. **HEAT** oven to 350°F. Roll dough to ⅛-inch thickness on lightly floured surface. Cut into assorted shapes, using 3-inch cookie cutters. Place, 2 inches apart, on greased baking sheets. Sprinkle with colored sugar.

3. **BAKE** 10 to 12 min. or until edges begin to brown. Cool on baking sheets 3 min.; transfer to wire racks. Cool completely.

CHOCO-ORANGE COOKIES:
Prepare dough as directed, adding 1 Tbsp. orange zest with the flour and baking soda. Shape into 2 (8-inch) logs; wrap in plastic wrap. Refrigerate 1 hour. Heat oven to 350°F. Unwrap logs; cut into ¼-inch-thick slices. Place on baking sheets. Bake 12 to 15 min. or until edges begin to brown. Cool on wire racks. Drizzle with 4 melted squares BAKER'S Semi-Sweet Chocolate; let stand until set. Makes 5 doz. or 30 servings, 2 cookies each.

SNOWMEN COOKIES:
Heat oven to 350°F. Prepare dough as directed; shape into equal number of ½-inch and 1-inch balls. (You should have about 44 of each size ball.) Using 1 small and 1 large ball for each snowman, place balls on baking sheet, with balls touching each other. Flatten to ¼-inch thickness with bottom of glass dipped in additional flour. Repeat with remaining dough. Bake 10 to 14 min. or until lightly browned. Cool on wire racks. Garnish as desired. Makes 22 servings, 2 cookies each.

pecan bars

PREP: 20 min. | TOTAL: 1 hour 35 min. (incl. refrigerating) | MAKES: 60 servings.

▶ what you need!

1 pkg. (8 oz.) PHILADELPHIA Cream Cheese, softened

1 cup (2 sticks) butter, softened, divided

1 cup granulated sugar

1 Tbsp. vanilla, divided

2¼ cups all-purpose flour

½ tsp. baking soda

2 eggs

1 cup packed brown sugar

⅔ cup light corn syrup

3 cups chopped PLANTERS Pecans

▶ make it!

1. **BEAT** cream cheese, ¾ cup butter, granulated sugar and 2 tsp. vanilla in large bowl with mixer until well blended. Add flour and baking soda; mix well. Refrigerate 30 min.

2. **HEAT** oven to 350°F. Press dough onto bottom of 15×10×1-inch pan. Bake 20 min. or until lightly browned. Meanwhile, melt remaining butter; pour into medium bowl. Add eggs, brown sugar, corn syrup and remaining vanilla; mix well. Stir in nuts.

3. **SPREAD** nut mixture over warm crust. Bake 20 to 25 min. or until topping is firm around the edges but still slightly soft in the center. Cool completely.

SIZE-WISE:
These tasty bars are great for serving at a holiday party or for sharing at a cookie exchange.

Everyday Desserts

TRIFLES, TORTES, OVEN-FREE DELIGHTS, AND MORE

simply sensational truffles

PREP: 15 min. | TOTAL: 1 hour 15 min. (incl. refrigerating) | MAKES: 18 servings, 2 truffles each.

▶ what you need!

2½ pkg. (8 squares each) BAKER'S Semi-Sweet Chocolate, divided

1 pkg. (8 oz.) PHILADELPHIA Cream Cheese, softened

Decorations: chopped PLANTERS COCKTAIL Peanuts, melted BAKER'S Semi-Sweet Chocolate or White Chocolate

▶ make it!

1. **MELT** 8 chocolate squares. Beat cream cheese with mixer until creamy. Blend in melted chocolate. Refrigerate until firm.

2. **SHAPE** into 36 balls. Place on waxed paper-covered baking sheet.

3. **MELT** remaining chocolate. Use fork to dip truffles in chocolate; return to baking sheet. Decorate, then refrigerate 1 hour.

SIZE-WISE:
Chocolate truffles are rolled in a variety of coatings for a sweet treat that is perfect for gift-giving or for serving on a special occasion.

SUBSTITUTE:
Prepare using BAKER'S White Chocolate.

SPECIAL EXTRA:
Sprinkle truffles with crushed peppermint candies in addition to, or instead of, the chopped peanuts and melted chocolate.

SPECIAL EXTRA:
Add 1 to 2 tsp. of your favorite extract, such as peppermint, rum or almond; or ¼ cup of your favorite liqueur, such as orange or raspberry, to the chocolate mixture before shaping into balls.

VARIATION:
Coat truffles with powdered sugar or unsweetened cocoa powder instead of dipping in the melted chocolate and sprinkling with coatings.

layered strawberry cheesecake bowl

PREP: 20 min. | TOTAL: 4 hours 20 min. (incl. refrigerating) | MAKES: 14 servings, ⅔ cup each.

▶ what you need!

3 cups sliced fresh strawberries

3 Tbsp. sugar

2 pkg. (8 oz. each) PHILADELPHIA Neufchâtel Cheese, softened

1½ cups cold milk

1 pkg. (3.4 oz.) JELL-O Vanilla Flavor Instant Pudding

2 cups thawed COOL WHIP LITE Whipped Topping, divided

2 cups frozen pound cake cubes (1 inch)

1 square BAKER'S Semi-Sweet Chocolate

▶ make it!

1. **COMBINE** berries and sugar; refrigerate until ready to use. Beat Neufchâtel with mixer until creamy. Gradually beat in milk. Add dry pudding mix; mix well.

2. **BLEND** in 1½ cups COOL WHIP. Spoon half into 2½-qt. bowl.

3. **TOP** with layers of cake, berries and remaining cream cheese mixture. Refrigerate 4 hours.

4. **MELT** chocolate; drizzle over trifle. Top with remaining COOL WHIP.

SPECIAL EXTRA:
Garnish with chocolate-covered strawberries just before serving.

NOTE:
You will need about half of a 10.75-oz. pkg. pound cake to get the 2 cups cake cubes needed to prepare this recipe.

SIZE-WISE:
Enjoy your favorite foods while keeping portion size in mind.

striped delight

PREP: 20 min. | TOTAL: 4 hours 40 min. (incl. refrigerating) | MAKES: 24 servings.

▶ what you need!

35 OREO Cookies

6 Tbsp. butter, melted

1 pkg. (8 oz.) PHILADELPHIA Cream Cheese, softened

¼ cup sugar

2 Tbsp. cold milk

1 tub (12 oz.) COOL WHIP Whipped Topping, thawed, divided

2 pkg. (3.9 oz. each) JELL-O Chocolate Instant Pudding

3¼ cups cold milk

▶ make it!

1. **PROCESS** cookies in food processor until fine crumbs form. Transfer to medium bowl; mix in butter. Press onto bottom of 13×9-inch dish. Refrigerate until ready to use.

2. **WHISK** cream cheese, sugar and 2 Tbsp. milk in medium bowl until blended. Stir in 1¼ cups COOL WHIP; spread over crust.

3. **BEAT** pudding mixes and 3¼ cups milk with whisk 2 min.; pour over cream cheese layer. Let stand 5 min. or until thickened; cover with remaining COOL WHIP. Refrigerate 4 hours.

SIZE-WISE:
Enjoy this dessert on a special occasion, but stick to the serving size of this rich treat.

HOW TO EASILY CUT INTO SQUARES:
Place dessert in freezer about 1 hour before cutting into squares to serve.

SPECIAL EXTRA:
Drizzle each plate with melted BAKER'S Semi-Sweet Chocolate before topping with dessert square. Sprinkle with crushed candy canes or additional crushed OREO Cookies.

make-ahead tiramisu

PREP: 20 min. | TOTAL: 24 hours 20 min. (incl. refrigerating) | MAKES: 12 servings.

▶ what you need!

2 Tbsp. MAXWELL HOUSE Instant Coffee

¼ cup boiling water

32 Reduced Fat NILLA Wafers

1 tub (8 oz.) PHILADELPHIA Neufchâtel Cheese

¼ cup powdered sugar

1 tub (8 oz.) COOL WHIP FREE Whipped Topping, thawed

1 cup fresh raspberries

1 tsp. unsweetened cocoa powder

▶ make it!

1. **STIR** coffee granules into boiling water until dissolved. Cover bottom of 8-inch square dish with 16 wafers. Drizzle with 1 Tbsp. coffee.

2. **ADD** 2 Tbsp. of the remaining coffee gradually to Neufchâtel in medium bowl, beating with whisk until blended. Add sugar; mix well. Stir in COOL WHIP; spoon half over wafers in dish. Cover with remaining wafers. Drizzle with remaining coffee; top with remaining cream cheese mixture.

3. **REFRIGERATE** overnight. Top with raspberries just before serving; sprinkle with cocoa powder.

NUTRITION BONUS:
This great-tasting version of a classic dessert, prepared with better-for-you products, can be part of a healthful eating plan.

chocolate mousse torte

PREP: 20 min. | TOTAL: 3 hours 20 min. (incl. refrigerating) | MAKES: 16 servings.

▸ what you need!

37 NILLA Wafers, divided

4 squares BAKER'S Semi-Sweet Chocolate, divided

2 pkg. (3.9 oz. each) JELL-O Chocolate Instant Pudding

2 cups plus 2 Tbsp. cold milk, divided

1 tub (8 oz.) COOL WHIP Whipped Topping, thawed, divided

1 pkg. (8 oz.) PHILADELPHIA Cream Cheese, softened

¼ cup sugar

¾ cup fresh raspberries

▸ make it!

1.

STAND 16 wafers around inside edge of 9-inch round pan lined with plastic wrap. Melt 3 chocolate squares as directed on package.

2.

BEAT pudding mixes and 2 cups milk in medium bowl with whisk 2 min. Add melted chocolate; mix well. Stir in 1 cup COOL WHIP; pour into prepared pan.

3.

BEAT cream cheese, sugar and remaining milk with mixer until well blended. Stir in 1 cup of the remaining COOL WHIP; spread over pudding. Top with remaining wafers. Refrigerate 3 hours.

4.

INVERT torte onto plate. Remove pan and plastic wrap. Shave remaining chocolate square into curls. Top torte with remaining COOL WHIP, berries and chocolate curls.

Make-Ahead Appetizers

COLD DIPS AND NIBBLES THAT CAN BE MADE IN ADVANCE

salsa roll-ups

PREP: 10 min. | TOTAL: 10 min. | MAKES: 10 servings.

▶ what you need!

4 oz. (½ of 8-oz. pkg.) PHILADELPHIA Neufchâtel Cheese, softened

3 Tbsp. TACO BELL® HOME ORIGINALS® Thick 'N Chunky Salsa

4 flour tortillas (6 inch)

½ cup KRAFT Mexican Style 2% Milk Finely Shredded Four Cheese

¼ tsp. chili powder

▶ make it!

1. **MIX** Neufchâtel and salsa; spread onto tortillas. Top with remaining ingredients.

2. **ROLL** up tortillas tightly. Cut each crosswise into 5 slices.

SPECIAL EXTRA:
Garnish with fresh cilantro leaves.

BLT ROLL-UPS:
Omit salsa, shredded cheese and chili powder. Spread tortillas with Neufchâtel as directed. Top evenly with 1 cup shredded lettuce, 2 Tbsp. OSCAR MAYER Bacon Pieces and 1 chopped tomato. Roll up and slice as directed.

MAKE AHEAD:
Prepare roll-ups as directed, but do not cut into slices. Tightly wrap each roll-up in plastic wrap. Refrigerate up to 4 hours. Slice just before serving.

TACO BELL® and HOME ORIGINALS® are trademarks owned and licensed by Taco Bell Corp.

PHILADELPHIA
creamy salsa dip

PREP: 5 min. | TOTAL: 5 min. | MAKES: 2 cups or 16 servings, 2 Tbsp. each.

▶ what you need!

1 pkg. (8 oz.) PHILADELPHIA Cream Cheese, softened

1 cup TACO BELL® HOME ORIGINALS® Thick 'N Chunky Salsa

▶ make it!

1. **MIX** ingredients until well blended.

2. **SERVE** with assorted cut-up fresh vegetables or tortilla chips.

SPECIAL EXTRA:
Top prepared dip with layers of 1 can (15 oz.) rinsed black beans and 1 cup of your favorite variety of KRAFT Mexican Style Finely Shredded Cheese.

PHILADELPHIA CREAMY BACON-RANCH DIP:
Prepare dip as directed, substituting ½ cup KRAFT Ranch Dressing for the salsa and stirring in ¼ cup OSCAR MAYER Real Bacon Bits with the dressing.

SUBSTITUTE:
Prepare using PHILADELPHIA Neufchâtel Cheese.

MAKE AHEAD:
Dip can be made ahead of time. Store in refrigerator until ready to serve.

MAKE YOUR OWN BAKED TORTILLA CHIPS:
Cut flour tortillas into desired shapes. Place in single layer on baking sheet. Bake at 350°F for 8 to 10 min. or until crisp. Cool on wire racks.

TACO BELL® and HOME ORIGINALS® are trademarks owned and licensed by Taco Bell Corp.

mexican layered dip

PREP: 10 min. | TOTAL: 1 hour 10 min. (incl. refrigerating) | MAKES: 5 cups or
40 servings, 2 Tbsp. each.

▶ what you need!

1 pkg. (8 oz.) PHILADELPHIA Neufchâtel Cheese, softened

1 Tbsp. TACO BELL® HOME ORIGINALS® Taco Seasoning Mix

1 cup TACO BELL® HOME ORIGINALS® Thick 'N Chunky Salsa

1 cup rinsed canned black beans

4 green onions, chopped

1 cup KRAFT 2% Milk Shredded Cheddar Cheese

1 cup shredded lettuce

2 Tbsp. sliced black olives

3 pkg. (13 oz. each) baked tortilla chips

▶ make it!

1. **BEAT** Neufchâtel with mixer until creamy. Add seasoning mix; mix well. Spread onto bottom of serving plate or 9-inch pie plate.

2. **TOP** with all remaining ingredients except chips.

3. **REFRIGERATE** 1 hour. Serve with chips.

MAKEOVER - HOW WE DID IT:
By preparing with Neufchâtel, KRAFT 2% Milk Shredded Cheddar Cheese and baked tortilla chips instead of regular products, you'll save 50 calories and 8 grams of fat per serving.

SPECIAL EXTRA:
Garnish with chopped fresh cilantro.

TACO BELL® and HOME ORIGINALS® are trademarks owned and licensed by Taco Bell Corp.

sun-dried tomato & garlic dip

PREP: 5 min. | TOTAL: 5 min. | MAKES: 2 cups or 16 servings, 2 Tbsp. each.

▶ what you need!

1 tub (8 oz.) PHILADELPHIA Cream Cheese Spread

½ cup MIRACLE WHIP Dressing

½ cup sun-dried tomatoes packed in oil, drained, chopped

2 Tbsp. finely chopped fresh chives

1 clove garlic, minced

1 tsp. black pepper

▶ make it!

1. **MIX** all ingredients until well blended.

2. **SERVE** with cut-up fresh vegetables or NABISCO Crackers, if desired.

MAKE AHEAD:
This dip can be made up to 24 hours in advance. The longer you leave this dip in the refrigerator, the better the flavor.

creamy crab and red pepper spread

PREP: 15 min. | TOTAL: 1 hour 15 min. (incl. refrigerating) | MAKES: 2¼ cups or 18 servings, 2 Tbsp. cheese spread and 5 crackers each.

▸ what you need!

2 green onions, thinly sliced, divided

1 tub (8 oz.) PHILADELPHIA Neufchâtel Cheese

1 can (6 oz.) lump crabmeat, drained

½ cup KRAFT 2% Milk Shredded Sharp Cheddar Cheese

½ cup finely chopped red bell peppers

1 Tbsp. GREY POUPON Dijon Mustard

RITZ Reduced Fat Crackers

▸ make it!

1. **REMOVE** 2 Tbsp. onions; set aside. Mix remaining onions with all remaining ingredients except crackers.

2. **REFRIGERATE** 1 hour.

3. **SPRINKLE** with reserved onions. Serve with crackers.

NUTRITION BONUS:
The red peppers provide flavor, color and a good source of vitamin C in this cheesy spread.

holiday cheese truffles

PREP: 15 min. | TOTAL: 4 hours 15 min. (incl. refrigerating) | MAKES: 4 doz. truffles or 24 servings, 2 truffles and 5 crackers each.

▶ what you need!

2 pkg. (8 oz. each) PHILADELPHIA Cream Cheese, softened

1 pkg. (8 oz.) KRAFT Shredded Sharp Cheddar Cheese

1 tsp. garlic powder

Dash ground red pepper (cayenne)

¼ cup chopped roasted red peppers

2 green onions, sliced

1⅔ cups chopped PLANTERS Pecans

SOCIABLES Savory Crackers

▶ make it!

1. **BEAT** first 4 ingredients with mixer until blended. Divide in half. Add roasted peppers to half and onions to other half; mix each until blended.

2. **REFRIGERATE** several hours or until chilled.

3. **SHAPE** into 48 (1-inch) balls. Roll in nuts. Refrigerate until ready to serve. Serve with crackers.

SIZE-WISE:
Enjoy a single serving of this indulgent holiday treat.

SPECIAL EXTRA:
Try these other coatings for a variety of tasty truffles: Sesame seeds, chopped fresh parsley, paprika or your favorite KRAFT Shredded Cheese.

VARIATIONS:
Prepare as directed, using one of the following options: **Festive Wreath**: Alternately arrange different flavored truffles in a large circle on platter to resemble a holiday wreath. Create a decorative bow out of green onion strips. Use to garnish wreath. **Cheese Logs**: Roll each half into 6-inch log. Roll in desired coatings as directed.

Hot & Savory
Appetizers

WARM AND CHEESY DIPS AND SMALL BITES

cream cheese-bacon crescents

PREP: 15 min. | TOTAL: 30 min. | MAKES: 16 servings.

▸ what you need!

1 tub (8 oz.) PHILADELPHIA Chive & Onion Cream Cheese Spread

3 slices OSCAR MAYER Bacon, cooked, crumbled

2 cans (8 oz. each) refrigerated crescent dinner rolls

▸ make it!

HEAT oven to 375°F.

1. **MIX** cream cheese spread and bacon until well blended.

2. **SEPARATE** each can of dough into 8 triangles. Cut each triangle lengthwise in half. Spread each dough triangle with 1 generous tsp. cream cheese mixture. Roll up, starting at shortest side of triangle; place, point-sides down, on baking sheet.

3. **BAKE** 12 to 15 min. or until golden brown. Serve warm.

HEALTHY LIVING:
For a reduced-fat version, prepare using PHILADELPHIA Chive & Onion ⅓ Less Fat than Cream Cheese and reduced-fat refrigerated crescent dinner rolls. As a bonus, these changes will save 30 calories per serving, too!

VARIATION:
For a sweet version, prepare using PHILADELPHIA Strawberry Cream Cheese Spread and substituting chopped PLANTERS Walnuts for the bacon.

make-ahead spinach phyllo roll-ups

PREP: 30 min. | TOTAL: 55 min. | MAKES: 30 servings or 5 logs, 6 servings each.

▶ what you need!

1 egg, beaten

1 pkg. (10 oz.) frozen chopped spinach, thawed, drained

1 cup ATHENOS Traditional Crumbled Feta Cheese

1 tub (8 oz.) PHILADELPHIA Garden Vegetable ⅓ Less Fat than Cream Cheese

4 green onions, finely chopped

15 sheets frozen phyllo (14×9 inch), thawed

⅓ cup butter, melted

▶ make it!

1. **MIX** first 5 ingredients until well blended; set aside. Brush 1 phyllo sheet lightly with butter; top with 2 more phyllo sheets, lightly brushing each layer with some of the remaining butter. Place remaining phyllo between sheets of plastic wrap; set aside.

2. **SPREAD** ⅕ of the spinach mixture along 1 short side of phyllo stack; fold in both long sides then roll up, starting at 1 of the short sides to make log. Repeat with remaining phyllo sheets and spinach mixture to make 4 more logs. Brush with remaining butter. Make small cuts in tops of logs at 1-inch intervals. Place in large freezer-weight resealable plastic bags or wrap tightly in plastic wrap.

3. **FREEZE** up to 3 months. When ready to bake, remove desired number of logs from freezer. Refrigerate, tightly wrapped, several hours or overnight until thawed. Unwrap, then place on baking sheet. Bake in 375°F oven 25 min. or until golden brown. Cool on baking sheet 5 min.; transfer to cutting board. Use serrated knife to cut each log into 6 slices.

STORAGE KNOW-HOW:
Leftover phyllo sheets can be wrapped tightly and refrozen.

HOW TO PREPARE WITH 18×14-INCH PHYLLO SHEETS:
Use a total of 9 phyllo sheets, spreading one-third of the filling on each stack of 3 sheets and rolling up each stack to make a total of 3 logs. Freeze and bake as directed. Cut each log into 10 slices to serve.

VARIATION:
Omit butter. Spray phyllo sheets with cooking spray instead of brushing with the melted butter.

fiesta baked cheese dip

PREP: 20 min. | TOTAL: 40 min. | MAKES: 4 cups or 32 servings, 2 Tbsp. each.

▶ what you need!

2 pkg. (8 oz. each) PHILADELPHIA Cream Cheese, softened

1 pkg. (8 oz.) KRAFT Mexican Style Finely Shredded Four Cheese, divided

1 can (4 oz.) chopped green chiles, undrained

1¼ cups BREAKSTONE'S or KNUDSEN Sour Cream, divided

¼ to ½ tsp. ground red pepper (cayenne)

▶ make it!

HEAT oven to 350°F.

1. **BEAT** cream cheese in large bowl with mixer until creamy. Reserve ¼ cup shredded cheese. Add remaining shredded cheese to cream cheese with chiles, ½ cup sour cream and ground red pepper; mix well.

2. **SPOON** into 10-inch pie plate or quiche dish.

3. **BAKE** 20 min. or until edge is lightly browned. Top with remaining sour cream and shredded cheese. Serve with tortilla chips.

SUBSTITUTE:
Substitute KRAFT Shredded Colby/Monterey Jack Cheese for Mexican Style Shredded Cheese.

SPECIAL EXTRA:
Assemble dip and bake as directed. Top with 2 Tbsp. chopped green onions or chopped fresh cilantro.

easy cheesy buffalo chicken dip

PREP: 10 min. | TOTAL: 15 min. | MAKES: about 2½ cups or 40 servings, 2 Tbsp. each.

▶ what you need!

1 pkg. (8 oz.) PHILADELPHIA Cream Cheese, cubed

1½ cups finely chopped cooked chicken

½ cup KRAFT ROKA Blue Cheese Dressing

½ cup hot pepper sauce for Buffalo wings

2 stalks celery, finely chopped

▶ make it!

1. **MIX** all ingredients in medium microwaveable bowl.

2. **MICROWAVE** on HIGH 5 min. or until cream cheese is melted and mixture is heated through, stirring after 3 min.

3. **SERVE** hot with WHEAT THINS Original Crackers or celery sticks.

SUBSTITUTE:
Substitute finely chopped OSCAR MAYER Deli Fresh Oven Roasted Chicken Breast Cuts or Grilled Chicken Breast Strips for the chopped cooked fresh chicken.

MAKE AHEAD:
Dip can be made ahead of time. Pour into small slow cooker or fondue pot to keep warm until ready to serve.

mini cream cheese and pepper jelly phyllo cups

PREP: 20 min. | TOTAL: 40 min. | MAKES: 3 doz. or 12 servings, 3 phyllo cups each.

▶ what you need!

6 frozen phyllo sheets, thawed

2 Tbsp. butter, melted

1 pkg. (8 oz.) PHILADELPHIA Cream Cheese, cut into 36 cubes

6 Tbsp. hot pepper jelly

▶ make it!

HEAT oven 350°F.

1. **BRUSH** 1 phyllo sheet with butter; top with second phyllo sheet. Brush top with butter; cut into 24 (2-inch) squares. Stack 2 squares, on an angle, to make 4 thicknesses; repeat with remaining phyllo sheets and butter. Press 1 stack into each of 36 miniature (1½-inch) muffin cups.

2. **ADD** 1 cream cheese cube to each cup. Bake 20 min. or until cream cheese is melted and pastry is golden brown.

3. **TOP** each serving with ½ tsp. hot pepper jelly.

SIZE-WISE:
Select a few of your favorite appetizers rather than sampling one of each to save room for your entrée.

STORAGE KNOW-HOW:
Leftover phyllo sheets can be wrapped tightly and refrozen until ready to use.

MAKE IT EASY:
Prepare as directed, using purchased jalapeño jelly.

Index